Healed by His Stripes

The key to divine health!

by

Florence Johnson

Editor:	**Esme James**
Cover design:	**Tanya Luke**

Blessed Unlimited Faith Ministries (BUFM)

www.bufm.net   *info@blessedltd.com*

Contents

By His Stripes We Are Healed

Healing Mini-Book

Receiving healing for your body is supposed to be very easy. The Lord created the body to repair itself when anything goes wrong with it. However, when medical science and other complicated sets of procedures came on the scene, it became a difficult, if not impossible feat for humanity to be healed without the use of one or the other. . The main reason for this is that man is operating only within the confines of the five senses and has no idea that the spiritual exists or that it is more real than the physical.

The bible teaches us that sickness and disease are a result of the curse caused by the fall of mankind when Adam and Eve sinned in the Garden of Eden. However, the curse was broken in the ultimate sacrifice of Jesus Christ. It follows then that any

3

disease in the body is an attack from the enemy; it can be healed by the spiritual knowledge of the price that Jesus paid with His body and precious blood!

Healing is in the atonement and Jesus would not have paid the price of His life for us if we were still meant to be seeking help apart from Him. Healing for our lives can now be obtained by appropriating the realities of the spiritual realm through the power of the Holy Spirit. Unfortunately, most Christians do not know how to walk in this reality and instead, like the world, turn to medical science rather than the Lord, through the power of the Holy Spirit.

Hopefully, this mini-book will bring some understanding of how to receive any form of healing, be it physical, financial, emotional or material, by developing a close relationship with the Lord. All the power we need to defeat any disease, resulting in ailments and sicknesses that torment believers, is in the name of Jesus and the power of the Holy Spirit and cannot be obtained otherwise! The reason being that, "God is Spirit, and those who worship Him must worship Him in spirit and in truth."" (John 4:24 NKJV). A Christian is to walk in the spirit by faith and not by sight (or any of our five senses). This does not mean our five senses are redundant; however, our sixth sense - our spirit – should dominate, control and dictate to all the others. We have to rely on our spirit to change any negative situation or circumstance. The body and soul have to conform to the Holy Spirit that is within us - that's where the power resides!

If you study the miracles in both the Old and New Testaments, everyone who believed was healed by faith and those who tried medical science either died prematurely, like King Asa in 2 Chronicles

16, or suffered greatly and even grew worse, like the woman with the issue of blood (Matthew 9, Mark 5 and Luke 8).

<u>Proviso</u>: the walk of faith is spiritual and totally dependent on believing the Word of God through an intimate relationship with Him . Where there's any doubt or unbelief you will not be able to receive the desired result and then it's best to seek medical help and continue to build your faith until you can totally rely on the Lord without medical intervention. Walking by faith goes beyond just stating that you're walking by faith, praying or confessing scriptures (these are important). However, total reliance on the Lord is a knowledge, a Rhema conviction and confidence in the power from within, that considers no other options. Jesus becomes your GP, your Surgeon and the Word of God –and nothing else – your medicine. It may seem as if this supernatural way takes longer than taking prescribed medication from doctors, but it has no side effects and your body (the Lord's temple), is not defiled by chemicals which have become idols for many Christians!

Also, God in His mercy, could work through the physicians, but many a time, they have been known to declare there's nothing else they can do and pronounce the death sentence! However, the One who raises the dead is always available and He declares in Psalm 118 that you shall not die but live to declare His works.

Your BODY: The Temple of the Lord

God being a Spirit created us in His image and after His likeness (Genesis 1:26-31). "And the Lord God formed man of the dust of the ground, and breathed into his nostrils the breath of life; and man became a living soul." (Genesis 2:7 KJV). Our bodies are an encasement, housing our spirit and that's why the Word confirms that the body without the spirit is dead; which means our spirit should control the house and not vice versa. God has created our body to repair itself and when there's an attack by sickness, you should, through your spirit, exercise its power and command the healing power from within to heal and strengthen the body.

In the New Testament we've been empowered by the truth that the Holy Spirit inhabits our bodies as His temple. What a privilege and an

honour for our bodies to be the sanctuary and tabernacle for the Lord as He dwells in us with all the power we need to live in this life. Paul explains this in Romans 8:11: "But if the Spirit of Him who raised Jesus from the dead dwells in you, He who raised Christ from the dead will also give life to your mortal bodies through His Spirit who dwells in you." (NKJV)

"Do you not know that you are the temple of God and that the Spirit of God dwells in you? If anyone **defiles** the temple of God, God will destroy him. For the temple of God is holy, which temple you are." (I Corinthians 3:16-17 NKJV)

"And what agreement has the temple of God with **idols**? For you are the temple of the living God. As God has said: "I will dwell in them And walk among them. I will be their God, And they shall be My people."" (2 Corinthians 6:16 NKJV)

"Foods for the stomach and the stomach for foods,
but God will destroy both it and them. Now the
body is not for **sexual immorality** but for the
Lord, and the Lord for the body."
(I Corinthians 6:13 NKJV)

"Flee sexual immorality. Every **sin** that a man does
is outside the body, but he who commits sexual
immorality sins against his own body. Or do you
not know that your body is the temple of the Holy
Spirit who is in you, whom you have from God,
and you are not your own? For you were bought at
a price; therefore glorify God in your body and in
your spirit, which are God's."
(I Corinthians 6:18-20 NKJV)

"I beseech you therefore, brethren, by the mercies
of God, that you present your bodies a living
sacrifice, holy, acceptable to God, which is your
reasonable service. And do not be conformed to
this world, but be transformed by the renewing of

your mind, that you may prove what is that good and acceptable and perfect will of God."
(Romans 12:1-2 NKJV)

"…for in Him we live and move and have our being, as also some of your own poets have said, 'For we are also His offspring.'"
(Acts 17:28 NKJV)

The Lord formed you and knows every part of your body - inside organs and outside tissues. There is nothing hidden from Him and He is aware of when something goes wrong; He can fix it since He created us. If only you can believe!

"For You formed my inward parts; You covered me in my mother's womb. I will praise You, for I am fearfully and wonderfully made; Marvellous are Your works, And that my soul knows very well. My frame was not hidden from You, When I

was made in secret, And skilfully wrought in the lowest parts of the earth. Your eyes saw my substance, being yet unformed. And in Your book they all were written, The days fashioned for me, When as yet there were none of them."
(Psalms 139:13-16 NKJV)

For He knows our frame; He remembers that we are dust." (Psalms 103:3-5, 14 NKJV)

With this knowledge, when there is a problem with the body, one should be communicating with the Creator, the Holy Spirit and not concentrating on the flesh and its feelings. For as a glove without the hand is useless or the body without a head is dead, so the body is dead without the spirit:

"But you are not in the flesh but in the Spirit, if indeed the Spirit of God dwells in you.… And if Christ is in you, the body is dead because of sin,

but the Spirit is life because of righteousness."
(Romans 8: 9-10 NKJV)

Also, if you depend on your feelings and live according to what the doctors say, you will die; but if you live according to the supernatural spirit of God you will surely live.

"For if you live according to the flesh you will die; but if by the Spirit you put to death the deeds of the body, you will live." (Romans 8:13 NKJV)

"For those who live according to the flesh set their minds on the things of the flesh, but those who live according to the Spirit, the things of the Spirit. For to be carnally-minded is death, but to be spiritually-minded is life and peace. So then, <u>those who are in the flesh cannot please God</u>."
(Romans 8:5-6, 8 NKJV)

"But without faith it is impossible to please Him, for he who comes to God must believe that He is, and that He is a rewarder of those who diligently seek Him." Hebrews 11:6 NKJV

In order to live by the spirit you have to crucify and put to death the flesh and its passions and allow Christ to live in you by faith; remember you are now a new creation: the old has passed away and you are now a new person in Christ.

"I have been crucified with Christ; it is no longer I who live, but Christ lives in me; and the life which I now live in the flesh I live by faith in the Son of God, who loved me and gave Himself for me." (Galatians 2:20 NKJV)

"And that He died for all, that they which live should not henceforth live unto themselves, but unto Him who died for them, and rose again. Wherefore henceforth know we no man after the

flesh: yea, though we have known Christ after the flesh, yet now henceforth know we Him no more. <u>Therefore if any man be in Christ, he is a new creature: old things are passed away; behold, all things are become new.</u>"
(2 Corinthians 5:15-17 KJV)

He died for everyone so that those who receive His new life will no longer live for themselves. Instead, **<u>they must live for Christ</u>**, who died and was raised for them.

So we have stopped evaluating others from a human point of view. At one time we thought of Christ merely from a human point of view. How differently we know him now! This means that anyone who belongs to Christ has become a new person. The old life is gone; a new life has begun! (2 Corinthians 5:15-17 NLT)

"From now on let no one trouble me, for <u>I bear in my body</u> the marks of the Lord Jesus."
(Galatians 6:17 NKJV)

"…in whom you also are being built together for a dwelling place of God in the Spirit."
(Ephesians 2:22 NKJV)

"For <u>**we are members of His body**</u>, of His flesh and of His bones." (Ephesians 5:30 NKJV)

"…according to my earnest expectation and hope that in nothing I shall be ashamed, but with all boldness, as always, so now also <u>**Christ will be magnified in my body**</u>, whether by life or by death. For to me, to live is Christ, and to die is gain." (Philippians 1:20-21 NKJV)

To them God willed to make known what are the riches of the glory of this mystery among the Gentiles: which is <u>**Christ in you the hope of glory**</u>. (Colossians 1:27)

<u>Food</u>

In recent times everyone has become more particular about the food they eat. Of course, we should eat good, fresh and well-cooked food, but the emphasis on food, diets and exercise has been blown out of proportion, to the point that doctors and dieticians are now the experts on what's best for our bodies instead of what the Creator of our bodies' states in His word!

Christians imbibe the doctrines of the world which we are warned against in Paul's letter to Timothy. In 1 Tim 4:1-5, he says that to be abstaining from meats created by God is tantamount to heeding seducing spirits and doctrines of devils!

"Now the Spirit expressly says that in latter times some will depart from the faith, giving heed to <u>deceiving spirits and doctrines of demons</u>, speaking lies in hypocrisy, having their own conscience seared with a hot iron, forbidding to marry, and **commanding to abstain from foods** which God created to be received with thanksgiving by those who believe and know the truth. For every creature of God is good, and nothing is to be refused if it is **received with thanksgiving; for it is sanctified by the word of God and prayer**." (I Timothy 4:1-5 NKJV)

"Not what goes into the mouth defiles a man; but what comes out of the mouth, this defiles a man." Watch what you are saying and listening to when there is a health challenge – this is what defiles and pollutes the body.

So Jesus said, "Are you also still without understanding? Do you not yet understand that whatever enters the mouth goes into the stomach and is eliminated? But those things which proceed out of the mouth come from the heart, and they defile a man. For out of the heart proceed evil

thoughts, murders, adulteries, fornications, thefts, false witness, blasphemies. These are the things which defile a man, but to eat with unwashed hands does not defile a man."'"
(Matthew 15:11, 16-20 NKJV)

"There is nothing that enters a man from outside which can defile him; but the things which come out of him, those are the things that defile a man, because they come from the heart.

So He said to them, "Are you thus without understanding also? Do you not perceive that whatever enters a man from outside cannot defile him, because it does not enter his heart but his stomach, and is eliminated, thus purifying all foods?" And He said, "What comes out of a man, that defiles a man. For from within, out of the heart of men, proceed <u>evil thoughts</u>, adulteries, fornications, murders, thefts, covetousness,

wickedness, deceit, lewdness, an evil eye, blasphemy, pride, foolishness. All these evil things come from within and defile a man.""
(Mark 7:15, 18-23 NKJV)

"Jesus said, "Are you being wilfully stupid? Don't you see that what you swallow can't contaminate you? It doesn't enter your heart but your stomach, works its way through the intestines, and is finally flushed." (That took care of dietary quibbling; Jesus was saying that all foods are fit to eat.)

He went on: "**<u>It's what comes out of a person that pollutes</u>**: obscenities, lusts, thefts, murders, adulteries, greed, depravity, deceptive dealings, carousing, mean looks, slander, arrogance, foolishness—all these are vomit from the heart. There is the source of your pollution.""
(Mark 7:18-23 MSG)

"A man's stomach shall be satisfied from the fruit of his mouth; from the produce of his lips he shall be filled. **Death and life** are in the power of the tongue, And those who love it will eat its fruit."
(Proverbs 18:20-21 NKJV)

"You are **snared by the words of your mouth**; You are taken by the words of your mouth."
(Proverbs 6:2 NKJV)

"But no man can tame the tongue. It is an unruly evil, full of deadly poison." (James 3:8 NKJV)

Evil thoughts lead to negative confessions – for out of the abundance of the heart the mouth speaks (Luke 6:45)

"For bodily exercise profits a little, **but godliness is profitable for all things**, having promise of the life that now is and of that which is to come."
(I Timothy 4:8 NKJV).

The Spirit Within You

It is imperative to understand that the power of God within the Christian is limitless. Our redemption was obtained by the priceless blood of Jesus and the Spirit that God has made us, when He breathed into man and made him a living soul:

"And the Lord God formed man of the dust of the ground, and breathed into his nostrils the breath of life; and man became a living soul."
(Genesis 2:7 KJV)

"The Spirit of God has made me, And the breath of the Almighty gives me life." (Job 33:4 NKJV)

"And I will pray the Father, and He will give you another Helper, that He may abide with you forever— the Spirit of truth, whom the world cannot receive, because it neither sees Him nor

knows Him; but you know Him, for He dwells with you and will be in you."
(John 14:16-17 NKJV).

The Amplified version describes the Holy Spirit as our Comforter, Counsellor, Helper, Intercessor, Advocate, Strengthner and Standby!
(John 14:16 AMP.)

"The Spirit of the LORD shall rest upon Him, The Spirit of wisdom and understanding, The Spirit of counsel and might, The Spirit of knowledge and of the fear of the LORD." (Isaiah 11:2 NKJV)

"You also, as living stones, are being built up a spiritual house, a holy priesthood, to offer up spiritual sacrifices acceptable to God through Jesus Christ." (I Peter 2:5 NKJV)

"Knowing that **you were not redeemed with corruptible things, like silver or gold**, from your aimless conduct received by tradition from your fathers, **but with the precious blood of Christ, as of a lamb without blemish and without spot;** having been born again, not of corruptible seed but incorruptible, through the word of God which lives and abides forever," (I Peter 1:18-19, 23 NKJV)

"The spirit of man is the candle of the Lord, searching all the inward parts of the belly."
(Proverbs 20:27 KJV)

"A merry heart does good, like medicine, But a broken spirit dries the bones."
(Proverbs 17:22 NKJV)

"For if I pray in a tongue, my spirit prays, but my understanding is unfruitful.....Therefore, brethren, desire earnestly to **prophesy**, and do not forbid to speak with tongues."
(I Corinthians 14:14, 39 NKJV)

"That He would grant you, according to the riches of His glory, to be strengthened with might through His Spirit in the inner man,"
(Ephesians 3:16 NKJV)

Your Flesh Vs. Your Spirit

Do not live according to your flesh. Your body should not be in charge of your life; it is your spirit that should command your body and your soul. However, you need to set your mind on the things of the spirit to achieve such a state of being. Delve into God's word and appropriate the power that is available to you. Your body can alert you, that something is wrong with it, but it is your spirit that can mend and deal with the problem.

"For those who live according to the flesh set their minds on the things of the flesh, but those who live according to the Spirit, the things of the Spirit. **For to be carnally-minded is death, but to be spiritually-minded is life and peace**. (Romans 8:5-6 NKJV)

"But you are not in the flesh but in the Spirit, if indeed the Spirit of God dwells in you. Now if anyone does not have the Spirit of Christ, he is not His. And if Christ is in you, the body is dead because of sin, but the Spirit is life because of righteousness. But if the Spirit of Him who raised Jesus from the dead dwells in you, He who raised Christ from the dead will also give life to your mortal bodies through His Spirit who dwells in you." (Romans 8:9-11 NKJV)

"For if you live according to the flesh you will die; but if by the Spirit you put to death the deeds of the body, you will live. For as many as are led by the Spirit of God, these are sons of God." (Romans 8:13-14 NKJV).

"It is the Spirit who gives life; the flesh profits nothing. The words that I speak to you are spirit, and they are life." (John 6:63 NKJV)

"For he who sows to his flesh will of the flesh reap corruption, but he who sows to the Spirit will of the Spirit reap everlasting life."
(Galatians 6:8 NKJV)

The Power of Life and Healing Within You

But if **the Spirit of Him who raised Jesus from the dead dwells in you**, He who raised Christ from the dead will also give life to your mortal bodies through His Spirit who dwells in you." (Romans 8:11 NKJV)

"It is the Spirit who gives life; the flesh profits nothing. The words that I speak to you are spirit, and they are life." (John 6:63 NKJV)

"The mystery which has been hidden from ages and from generations, but now has been revealed to His saints. To them God willed to make known what are the riches of the glory of this mystery among the Gentiles: which is **Christ in you, the hope of glory."** (Colossians 1:26-27 NKJV)

"And not holding fast to the Head, from whom all the body, nourished and knit together by joints and ligaments, grows with the increase that is from God." (Colossians 2:19 NKJV)

"But you have an anointing from the Holy One, and you know all things.

But **the anointing which you have received from Him abides in you**, and you do not need that anyone teach you; but as the same anointing teaches you concerning all things, and is true, and is not a lie, and just as it has taught you, you will abide in Him." (I John 2:20, 27 NKJV)

"You are of God, little children, and have overcome them, because **He who is in you is greater than he who is in the world.**"
(I John 4:4 NKJV)

"Have you not known? Have you not heard? The everlasting God, the LORD, The Creator of the ends of the earth, neither faints, nor is weary. His understanding is unsearchable. **He gives power to the weak**, And to those who have no might He increases strength." (Isaiah 40:28-29 NKJV)

"A man's stomach shall be satisfied from the fruit of his mouth; from the produce of his lips he shall be filled. **Death and life are in the power of the tongue**, And those who love it will eat its fruit." (Proverbs 18:20-21 NKJV)

"Beloved, I pray that you may prosper in all things and **be in health**, just as your soul prospers." (3 John 1:2 NKJV)

"[He] forgives all your iniquities, **[He] heals all your diseases**, [He] redeems your life from destruction, [He] crowns you with lovingkindness and tender mercies, [He] satisfies your mouth with good things, So that your youth is renewed like the eagle's. (Psalms 103:3-5 NKJV)

"Then they cried out to the LORD in their trouble, and He saved them out of their distresses. **He sent His word and healed them**, and delivered them from their destructions."
(Psalms 107:19-20 NKJV)

"As **His divine power has given to us all things that pertain to life and godliness,** through the knowledge of Him who called us by glory and virtue, by which have been given to us exceedingly great and precious promises, that through these you may **be partakers of the divine nature**, having escaped the corruption that is in the world through lust." (2 Peter 1:3-4 NKJV.)

"That the God of our Lord Jesus Christ, the Father of glory, **may give to you the spirit of wisdom and revelation in the knowledge of Him, the eyes of your understanding being enlightened**; that you may know what is the hope of His calling, what are the riches of the glory of His inheritance in the saints, and what is the exceeding greatness of His power toward us who believe, according to the working of His mighty power which He worked in Christ when He raised Him from the dead and seated Him at His right hand in the heavenly places, far above all principality and power and might and dominion, and every name that is named, not only in this age but also in that which is to come." (Ephesians 1:17-21 NKJV)

"But God, who is rich in mercy, because of His great love with which He loved us, even when we were dead in trespasses, made us alive together with Christ (by grace you have been saved), and raised us up together, and made us **sit together in the heavenly places in Christ Jesus,**" (Ephesians 2:4-6 NKJV)

"Examine yourselves as to whether you are in the faith. Test yourselves. Do you not know yourselves, **that Jesus Christ is in you**?—unless indeed you are disqualified."

(2 Corinthians 13:5 NKJV.)

"Either make the tree good and its fruit good, or else make the tree bad and its fruit bad; for a tree is known by *its* fruit. Brood of vipers! How can you, being evil, speak good things? For **out of the abundance of the heart the mouth speaks.** A good man out of the good treasure of his heart brings forth good things, and an evil man out of the evil treasure brings forth evil things. But I say to you that for every idle word men may speak, they will give account of it in the day of judgment. **For by your words you will be justified, and by your words you will be condemned.**" (Matthew 12:33-37. NKJV.)

How to Appropriate the Healing Power in Your Spirit

The word of God is spirit and life (John 6:63). When your body is weak or there are evil symptoms, don't panic and say the wrong things or begin to self diagnose – SPEAK THE WORD! Dictate to the issue and command it to leave! If it persists you then go into warfare and counter attack with the name of Jesus, the blood, the word and praying in other tongues!

Control your thoughts:

Thinking and thoughts have a definite effect your body. If your mind is focused on weariness, sickness, fear etc, your body mechanism will respond to such suggestions. This is because your mind has direct control over your nervous system, glands, muscles, heart, blood pressure etc.

Thus, how you think you feel has a direct impact and effect upon how you actually feel. If your mind is stayed on God you will experience peace. "You will keep him in perfect peace, whose mind is stayed on You, because he trusts in You." (Isaiah 26:3 NKJV).

When you are quiet and evil thoughts come into your mind to make you afraid, know they come from the devil and you need to cast out every such imagination.

Casting down imaginations and every high thing that exalteth itself against the knowledge of God, and bringing into captivity every thought to the obedience of Christ; (2 Cor. 10:5. KJV)

Do not walk in fear:

For God has not given us a spirit of fear, but of power and of love and of a sound mind.
(2 Timothy 1:7. NKJV)

"My son, let them not depart from your eyes—
Keep sound wisdom and discretion; So they will
be life to your soul And grace to your neck. Then
you will walk safely in your way, and your foot
will not stumble. **When you lie down, you will
not be afraid; yes, you will lie down and your
sleep will be sweet. Do not be afraid of sudden
terror, nor of trouble from the wicked when it
comes;** For the LORD will be your confidence,
And will keep your foot from being caught. Do not
withhold good from those to whom it is due, when
it is in the power of your hand to do so. Do not say
to your neighbour, "Go, and come back, and
tomorrow I will give it," When you have it with
you." (Proverbs 3:21-28 NKJV)

Train and exercise your body to conform to your spirit and do not be anxious

"I say then: Walk in the Spirit, and you shall not fulfil the lust of the flesh. For the flesh lusts against the Spirit, and the Spirit against the flesh; and these are contrary to one another, so that you do not do the things that you wish. But if you are led by the Spirit, you are not under the law.

And those who are Christ's have crucified the flesh with its passions and desires."
(Galatians 5:16-18, 24 NKJV)

Remember that Jesus your GP lives in you

"And Jesus went about all Galilee, teaching in their synagogues, preaching the gospel of the kingdom, and <u>healing all kinds of sickness and all kinds of disease</u> among the people."
(Matthew 4:23. NKJV)

"The spirit of a man will sustain him in sickness,

But who can bear a broken spirit?"

(Proverbs 18:14 NKJV)

"But those who wait on the LORD shall renew their strength; they shall mount up with wings like eagles, They shall run and not be weary, They shall walk and not faint." (Isaiah 40:31 NKJV)

Remember you are a new person in Christ

"[See] that you put off, concerning your former conduct, the old man which grows corrupt according to the deceitful lusts, and be renewed in the spirit of your mind, and that you put on the new man which was created according to God, in true righteousness and holiness." (Ephesians 4:22-24 NKJV).

"But ye are a chosen generation, a royal priesthood, an holy nation, a peculiar people; that ye should shew forth the praises of Him who hath called you out of darkness into his marvellous light:

Who His own self bare our sins in his own body on the tree, that we, being dead to sins, should live unto righteousness: **by whose stripes ye were healed.**" (1 Peter 2:9, 24 KJV)

"Whether Paul or Apollos or Cephas, or the world or life or death, or things present or things to come—all are yours. And **you are Christ's, and Christ is God's.**" (I Corinthians 3:22-23 NKJV)

<u>Pray in the spirit</u>

"But you, beloved, building yourselves up on your most holy faith, praying in the Holy Spirit, keep yourselves in the love of God, looking for the mercy of our Lord Jesus Christ unto eternal life." (Jude 1:20-21 NKJV)

Take communion with reverence

"So anyone who eats this bread or drinks this cup of the Lord unworthily is guilty of sinning against the body and blood of the Lord. That is why you should examine yourself before eating the bread and drinking the cup. For if you eat the bread or drink the cup without honouring the body of Christ, you are eating and drinking God's judgment upon yourself. That is why many of you are weak and sick and some have even died."
(1 Corinthians 11:27-30 NLT)

Watch your words

 "A man's stomach shall be satisfied from the fruit of his mouth; From the produce of his lips he shall be filled. **Death and life are in the power of the tongue,** and those who love it will eat its fruit."
(Proverbs 18:20-21 NKJV)

"You are **snared by the words of your mouth**; you are taken by the words of your mouth." (Proverbs 6:2 NKJV).

"My son, **attend to my words; incline thine ear unto my sayings.** Let them not depart from thine eyes; keep them in the midst of thine heart. For they are life unto those that find them, and health to all their flesh. Keep thy heart with all diligence; for out of it are the issues of life. Put away from thee a froward mouth, and perverse lips put far from thee. Let thine eyes look right on, and let thine eyelids look straight before thee. Ponder the path of thy feet, and let all thy ways be established. Turn not to the right hand nor to the left: remove thy foot from evil." (Proverbs 4:20-27 KJV).

Know your enemy

"The thief does not come except to steal, and to kill, and to destroy. I have come that they may

have life, and that they may have it more abundantly." (John 10:10 NKJV)

Be joyful

"A merry heart does good, like medicine, But a broken spirit dries the bones."
(Proverbs 17:22 NKJV).

Speak to your mountain

"For assuredly, I say to you, whoever says to this mountain, 'Be removed and be cast into the sea,' and **does not doubt in his heart**, but believes that those things he says will be done, he will have whatever he says. Therefore I say to you, whatever things you ask when you pray, believe that you receive them, and you will have them."
(Mark 11:23-24 NKJV).

"And these signs will follow those who **believe**: In My name they will cast out demons; they will speak with new tongues; they will take up

serpents; and if they drink anything deadly, it will by no means hurt them; **they will lay hands on the sick, and they will recover.'"**
(Mark 16:17-18 NKJV)

<u>Use your authority and declare the word</u>
"Behold, I give you the authority to trample on serpents and scorpions, and over all the power of the enemy, and nothing shall by any means hurt you." (Luke 10:19 NKJV).

"If you diligently heed the voice of the LORD your God and do what is right in His sight, give ear to His commandments and keep all His statutes, I will put none of the diseases on you which I have brought on the Egyptians. For I *am* the LORD who heals you." (Exodus 15:26. NKJV)

"Because you have made the LORD, who is my refuge, Even the Most High, your dwelling place, No evil shall befall you, Nor shall any plague

come near your dwelling;”
(Psalms 91:9-10 NKJV).

“No weapon formed against you shall prosper, And every tongue which rises against you in judgment You shall condemn. This is the heritage of the servants of the LORD, And their righteousness is from Me,” Says the LORD.” (Isaiah 54:17 NKJV)

“I shall not die, but live, and declare the works of the LORD.” (Psalms 118:17 NKJV)

Be relentless

Bind the powers of darkness and resist the enemy relentlessly until he flees from you! (James 4:7). Do not change your confession (Heb 10:23) nor become double minded (James 1:8; 4:8)
Walk in total faith and dependence on the Lord, without reservation and lean not on your understanding. (Proverbs 3:5-8)

Conclusion

Whatever you sow in **words, thoughts and beliefs** is what you will reap. You were not made to be sick, your body is meant to repair itself when there is an attack; however, if you do not resist the enemy he will not flee from you. Death and life are in the power of your tongue; therefore, speak life to your body and you will receive life. If you continue saying what the doctors say then you would have the results from their reports!

God has given us the power to decide what we want in life; when it comes to healing of our bodies the healing power is in our spirit and on our tongue! As Christians we are not meant to be sick nor are we to die sick; we should decide when we want to go home and be with our Father in heaven and at a ripe old age or when we have finished our race. Christians who want to stay alive, should not die, because the devil overpowers the body and kills it through sickness!

Most Christians die prematurely because of two things: first the **lack of knowledge**: the Bible says in Hosea 4:6, that people perish because of lack of knowledge; secondly, **they give up the fight** - Proverbs 24:10 asserts: "If thou faint in the day of adversity, thy strength is small."

Jude, the prophet said: "I have to write insisting—begging!—that you **fight with everything you have in you for this faith** entrusted to us as a gift to guard and cherish." (Jude 3 MSG)

And Paul, in his letter to Timothy advices him to, **"Fight the good fight of faith**, lay hold on eternal life, to which you were also called and have confessed the good confession in the presence of many witnesses." (1 Timothy 6:12)

Elisha died sick even though he had the power in his bones to stay alive. This must have been due either to a lack of knowledge, which we now have in the New Testament, or he gave up the fight. (See 2 Kings 13:14-21).

As believers we are called to fight the good fight of faith and having done all, we are to remain standing (victorious); we are living in evil days and our battle is not against flesh and blood but against the devil, demons and evil spirits!

Finally, my brethren, be strong in the Lord, and in the power of his might. Put on the whole armour of God that ye may be able to stand against the **wiles of the devil.** For we wrestle not against flesh and blood, but against principalities, against powers, against the rulers of the darkness of this world, against spiritual wickedness in high places. Wherefore take unto you the whole armour of God that ye may be able to withstand in the **evil**

day, and **having done all, to stand**. Stand therefore, having your loins girt about with truth, and having on the breastplate of righteousness; and your feet shod with the preparation of the gospel of peace; above all, taking the shield of faith, wherewith ye shall be able to quench all the fiery darts of the wicked. And take the helmet of salvation, and the sword of the Spirit, which is the word of God: Praying always with all **prayer and supplication in the Spirit**, and watching thereunto with all perseverance and supplication for all saints…. (Eph. 6:10-18 NKJV)

God is strong, and he wants you strong. So take everything the Master has set out for you, well-made weapons of the best materials. And put them to use so you will be able to stand up to everything the devil throws your way. This is no afternoon athletic contest that we'll walk away from and forget about in a couple of hours. This is for keeps

– a life-or-death fight to the finish against the devil and his demons.

Be prepared. You're up against far more than you can handle on your own. Take all the help you can get, every weapon God has issued, so that when all but the shouting is over, you'll still be on your feet. Truth, righteousness, peace, faith, and salvation are more than words. Learn how to apply them. You'll need them throughout your life. God's Word is an *indispensable* weapon. In the same way, prayer is essential in this ongoing warfare. Pray hard and long. Pray for your brothers and sisters. Keep your eyes open. Keep each other's spirits up so that no one falls behind or drops out. (Eph. 6:10-18 MSG).

Healing, Health and Happiness

Daily confessions:

You should apply the Word of God, the same way others take their physical medicine – morning, afternoon and evening. Do so without fail and with the same diligence that others follow the prescriptions of their doctors. The difference between physical medicine and spiritual medicine is that you don't have to wait until you begin to experience symptoms before you begin trying to get your healing. In fact, if you take them consistently, even when you don't have any symptoms, you will never get symptoms. The Word of God heals you before you need healing!

Morning tablets:

1. The same Spirit that raised Jesus from the dead dwells in me and quickens my mortal body – the Holy Spirit makes my body well! (See Rom. 8:11)

2. Why art thou cast down, O my soul? And why art thou disquieted within me? Hope thou in God: for I shall yet praise Him, who is the health of my countenance, and my God. (Psalms 42:11 KJV)

3. He sent his word, and healed me, and delivered me from my destructions. (Psalms 107:20 KJV)

4. With long life will [God Almighty] satisfy me and shew me his salvation. (Psalms 91:16 KJV)

5. My soul, wait thou only upon God; for my expectation is from him. He only is my rock and my salvation: he is my defence; I shall not be moved. In God is my salvation and my

glory: the rock of my strength, and my refuge, is in God. (Psalms 62:5-7 KJV)

Midday Tablets :

1. But He was wounded for [my] transgressions, He was bruised for [my] iniquities: the chastisement of [my] peace was upon Him; and with His stripes [I] am healed. (Isaiah 53:5 KJV)
2. Who His own self bore [my] sins in His own body on the tree, that [I], being dead to sins, should live unto righteousness: **by whose stripes [I] was healed**.
   (1 Peter 2:24 KJV)
3. I am beloved and above all things I prosper and in health, even as my soul prospereth. (3 John 1:2 KJV)
4. Lord my God, I cried unto thee, and thou hast healed me. (Psalms 30:2 KJV)

5. Heal me, O Lord, and I am healed; save
    me, and I am saved: for thou art my praise.
    (Jeremiah 17:14 KJV)

Night-time Tablets :

1. And Jesus went forth, and saw a great
    multitude, and was moved with compassion
    toward them, and he healed their sick.
    (Matthew 14:14) KJV)

2. Now when the sun was setting, all they that
    had any sick with divers diseases brought
    them unto him; and he laid his hands on
    every one of them, and healed them.
    (Luke 4:40 KJV)

3. I will not forget the Lord's law; but let my
    heart keep His commandments: For length
    of days, and long life, and peace, they add
    to me. (Proverbs 3:1-2 KJV)

4. [I] trust in the Lord with all [my] heart; and
    lean not unto [my] own understanding. In

all [my] ways [I] acknowledge Him, and He shall direct [my] paths. [I] shall not be wise in [my] own eyes: but [shall] fear the LORD, and depart from evil. It shall be health to [my] navel, and marrow to [my] bones. (Proverbs 3:5-8 KJV)

5. And as Jesus instructs, I have faith in God: [I] say unto this mountain of sickness, "Be thou removed, and be cast into the sea!" [I] have no doubt in [my] heart, but I believe that as [I] have spoken, so shall it come to pass and [I] shall have whatever [I] said. What things [I] desire, when [I] pray, [I] believe that [I] receive them, and I shall have them. And when [I] stand praying, [I] forgive, if [I] have anything against anyone: that [my] Father also which is in heaven may forgive [me my] trespasses. But if [I] do not forgive, neither will [my]

Father which is in heaven forgive [my] trespasses. (Mark 11:22-26 KJV)

6. **I resist the enemy of sickness and disease and it is well with my soul! I eat well and enjoy my food making me whole, healthy and happy in Jesus name.**

7. I lie down to sleep; I will awake in the morning, for the LORD sustains me.
    (Psalm 3:5)

8. "I shall not die, but live, and declare the works of the LORD."
    (Psalms 118:17 NKJV)

Daily Physical Necessities for the Body

G – Good fresh food, vegetables & fruits

R – Rest and relaxation

A – Air and sunshine

C – Clean and fresh water

E – Eat less, exercise more

Pray over all your organs and systems of your body; cover your life with the blood of Jesus and worship Him for making you live in divine health.

For You formed <u>my inward parts</u>; You covered me in my mother's womb. I will praise You, for I am <u>fearfully and wonderfully made</u>; marvellous are Your works, and that, my soul knows very well. <u>My frame</u> was not hidden from You; when I was made in secret, and <u>skilfully wrought</u> in the lowest pars of the earth. Your eyes saw <u>my substance</u> being yet unformed...(Psalms 139:13-16a)

1. My Circulatory System

2. My Digestive System

3. My Endocrine System

4. My Nervous System

5. My Respiratory System

6. My Urinary System

7. My Ears

8. My Muscles

9. My Bones

10. My Skin

11. My Brain

12. My Heart

13. My Spleen and pancreas

14. My Reproductive Organs

15. My Hands

16. My Teeth, Gums and Tongue

17. My Eyes,

BLESS HIS HOLY NAME! Bless the LORD, O
my soul, and forget not all his benefits.
(Psalms 103:1-2. KJV.)

<u>My healing journal</u>

<u>My healing cabinet (scriptures)</u>

<u>1.</u>

<u>2.</u>

<u>3.</u>

<u>4.</u>

<u>5.</u>

<u>6.</u>

Record of overcoming health challenges with the word – by speaking to the mountain:

PROBLEM	HOW YOU OVERCAME

	61

www.ingramcontent.com/pod-product-compliance
Lightning Source LLC
Chambersburg PA
CBHW031427250726